UNDER THE
INFLUENCE
OF YOUR CONTRAST
LEADING-EDGE
THINKERS

Finally a Great Way to
Feel Your Way to Happiness
*and Create the Dream You
are Meant to Live*

LUIS C. DELGADO

www.selfpublishn30days.com

Published by *Self Publish -N- 30 Days*

Copyright 2019 Luis C. Delgado.

Cover design by Patti Knoles, Virtual Graphic Arts Department

Printed in the United States of America

ISBN: 978-1-70847-224-5

1. Self-Help 2. Happiness 3. Growth 4. Emotional Intelligence

Luis C. Delgado
UNDER THE INFLUENCE OF YOUR CONTRAST LEADING-EDGE THINKERS

Disclaimer/Warning:

This book is intended for lecture and informative purposes only. This publication is designed to provide competent and reliable information regarding the subject matter covered. The author or publisher are not engaged in rendering legal or professional advice. Laws vary fro state to state and if legal, financial, or other expert assistance is needed, the services of a professional should be sought. The author and publisher disclaim any liability that is incurred from the use or application of the contents of this book.

DEDICATION

For the readers who are desiring to see something different in their life, and how thinking will provide a different perspective and getting what they want by knowing how to be.

I want to shout-out the family of Darren M. Palmer and entire staff for making this book come true again. I appreciate the guidance and support to allow me to share with the world, even if it is in my city only. What matters is that I am writing it. Thank you, Tricia Harris, for looking over my punctuation and some errors or mistakes and being the eyes to putting these sentences together. YOU are wonderful and I'm glad to have you as a great friend!

Thanks to Abraham-Hicks and Ester for allowing me to understand what it takes to learn about the Law of Attraction and for me to see what I need to see for my expansion of my life and co-create with everyone that I encounter. It is never over.

TABLE OF CONTENTS

ACKNOWLEDGEMENTS

I appreciate my number one mom for her support and love for me. I appreciate my brothers Pedro and Pierre for always letting me know that I am making a difference in my life, and how they are seeing things in a different point of view. How I am learning from their way, and how they are venturing their life.

My wonderful children Daniel and Ailani for being a key stone of life and how I am looking at you and see your life as an opportunity to excel and expand your wants.

My cousin Charly for being open and understanding how life is but how it could be.

My sister Ale for calling me your bro, making me feel wonderful, and how I appreciate you to the fullest.

The Echaverry family for staying true for being a loving, caring, and supportive family for all of us. For the Delgado's family of your love and excitement of life and how you live the life you want through your contrast of your own life.

Martha Marin for her experience and knowledge; and how we talk back and forth on how life brings us what we desire – and how much fun it is to receive it.

Of course, my deepest appreciation goes out to Jeena Vinayan for being there and helping me out every way possible. I am your fan of joy!

PREFACE

We interpret life based on our physical senses of Taste, Touch, Smell, Hear, and Feel and that is our perspective. We are the creator of our life. We live by default from others' point of view, and we say we think it's because we are different, or because we rebel at a certain point of our life and then we truly believe we are different.

I am here to explain how to fine tune "you" and how to influence you to be that version who you really are. Give birth to that desire you want in life. No one has taken your birth right of who you could be - or who you are. Today is your opportunity to start what you want to begin. You make the decision. Your true inner being is a lover, so when you see the opposite of something you do not like - you question or criticize their behavior because you are looking at them differently.

If you ask your inner being who you truly are, you will get back to your alignment of who you were meant to be. We are hard with one another. Mind your business, focus on who you are, send positive words or find a positive quality of that person, and you will see how you will change your feelings toward them.

Your bad choices show you where you are, and when you are misaligned with who you really are. The music you hear is the emotion of feeling and how you feel; yes, you are feeling what you are hearing, yes that means you are resonating what you are attracting – If that's happy or sad. What's your purpose? It is to be joyful! It is to be happy! It is who you are; it is how you feel!

You are here to explore who you are, and your expansion is secondary to the material you will get, and taste, and feel, and see in the experiences. As you start to focus on you and concentrate on your senses and their related emotions, you will see that this and know it is all an inside job.

INTRODUCTION

Are you ready to be ready to be ready? You know - I was thinking - the beautiful thing about life is that there is contrast. We have positive and negative. To see or feel what we want. And it allows us to move forward in the life that we want to create.

The people around us help us in a positive or negative way to finding who we are and what we want to become. I want to start off sharing the experiences I had which led to writing this book and how much it means to me. As a young man I was in a chain-of-confusion – not in pain, but in some emotional discomfort with a little pain because I allowed it.

I was just wondering why certain things worked and some didn't. Why was I feeling like a failure? Was this normal? Maybe I was meant to fail and continue the path of confusion and live the life that was presented to me. Maybe I was meant to look at everyone else enjoy their fabulous life and journey.

I wondered why there was a battle of events and why I allowed certain conditions or circumstances to bother me. My responses were negative, and I couldn't grab a hold of the feelings that were plaguing me daily.

When I was 12 years old, I felt I wasn't brilliant or smart or however you want to categorize my behavior; I felt I lost my inspiration and I needed to figure out where it went. All I was doing was following the crowd and not thinking clearly about my actions.

I kept doing the opposite of what life really meant for me to do. I was fighting an internal battle. There was a disconnection of who I really was. As I continued to look for my answers, I started to see more unwanted things happening in my life. I needed to figure it out and what direction to take to get greater clarity.

I was held back in the Sixth grade and expelled in Eighth grade for carrying weed (marijuana) in my backpack. The school staff finally had enough of my unwanted behavior. I didn't finish high school then because I felt fear, boredom, and confusion about who I really was.

At that time, the only option was to work. As I found odd jobs, I still wasn't happy. There was a temporary happiness when the money I was making came in (not like it was a lot) and I knew that wasn't the answer in my life.

I wanted more money. I wanted to make more money – but how? We will talk about that later. A lot of questions started to surface such as "What am I creating here?" In my pursuit to find a better idea, I started to look for God. Who is God? What did it mean to find Him – or just find something? Can I find God?

I was raised a Catholic, and I did the "First Communion" and attended the Sunday masses. Soon after I became an adult, I stopped going to the Catholic church. I wasn't tuned into that frequency, so I moved on.

We were living in Astoria Queens, 26-45 9th street; I remember getting a knock on our door, and it was the Jehovah's Witness people. They were ready to share their understanding, and I was ready to receive their teaching. I didn't question their faith. All I was looking for was answers.

There were too many rules and regulations with the Jehovah's Witnesses that didn't sit well with me; so, I continued to look and change direction. Years later, I attended a Pentecostal Sunday worship, and found it was not a fit for my answers either.

Then I learned about another Christian faith church and went there. It was a learning experience. I learned from their teaching, and I participated in Bible studies and lessons to understand the God they honored and followed. I even attended Seventh Day Adventist services and studied their faith and learned what they believe in.

Each one said it was superior to the others and I often speculated about why it was better and how so. Some people never looked outside the box or tried understanding the other churches. They were just so locked into their faith and belief, with no questions asked.

Considering it all was an experience for me. I loved all people and it didn't matter what faith they were in. I just couldn't understand the disconnection between love and all these different faiths. All I knew was that if people were in alignment with who they are, there would be no such thought of "We are better than them." That is why there is discord.

I didn't care what faith they followed. If the church folks helped the people in the church, made them feel loved, and changed them to be better, more power to them. I didn't think it mattered where they worshiped, as long as they were in a place where they showed love and taught how to think and be unconditional with others.

Now, I was asking why there were differences and disharmony in each one? I appreciated the time I took learning from each one's faith, how it impacted me in my life and how I see things in a difference perspective. My knowledge is knowing how to use my physical senses: touch, smell, see, hear, and taste. It is basic. It is simple.

Once you get the idea of using the senses you can start to create your life. I learned that life is a contrast to understanding the difference of wanted and unwanted; positive or negative; up or down, and how to get better at operating in the right emotional feeling.

Those experiences showed me what not to do. I started to focus on my WANT in life and how to expand. A belief is only a thought I keep thinking. A belief is only my habit of thought; it's only a practiced thought – a belief is only a thought that I think a lot.

We have physical senses that we use daily. Your eyes communicate and therefore you have the sense of sight. Your ears communicate and therefore you have sense of hearing. Your nose communicates and therefore you have the sense of smell. Your skin communicates and therefore you have the sense of feeling. Your tongue communicates and therefore you have the sense of taste.

When I picked up the book "Think and Grow Rich" by Napoleon Hill, I wasn't sure what to expect - all I wanted was to learn how to think and learn how to be better. When I continued to read and digest what Napoleon Hill was sharing, I started to find some of the answers of life. He mentions conscious, subconscious, and infinite intelligence.

When I first read it, I failed to grab his meaning. As I continued to re-read, I got the message about my life, and how to be successful in all areas of my life. I learned how I have infinite potential and mental faculty. That was the start of my learning.

I am always striving to expand my understanding and knowledge base. One night I was talking to my brother Pedro, and he mentioned "The Secret". We were going back and forth about the law of attraction, but I couldn't remember the movie, so I decided to watch it again.

When I watched it, I needed to figure something out, so I decided to look into Bob Proctor; he was in the movie, but something told me to search for him for greater understanding. I watched his YouTube video on "You were Born Rich." It was a nine-hour video. As I started to watch him and hear his message, he started to bring some perspective to my understanding, and I started to feel this zap or tingling in my body.

He introduced concepts about the conscious, subconscious, and mental faculties such as: Memory, Will, Perception, Imagination, Reason, and Intuition. For sure, he cleared and uncluttered some beliefs I'd thought my whole life. I re-watched those videos for 30 days over and over and over. That was recommended and I watched, because I was following my instinct.

From that moment on, I realized certain things about life and how I should be able to learn and not allow, by default, the things that were holding me back from pursuing what I was meant to be.

Let's continue and build understanding about what this "contrast" is all about and why we need both positive and negative aspects to be part of our daily life – and about not getting so caught up with it.

CHAPTER 1

Telling an Old Story

*If the ideas are negative,
they will – in turn – create negative results.*

Are we under the influence of our old story? A negative energy in our life? Are we not influenced by others? [Scratching head…] You are exercising complaints, worries, feeling unimportant, gossip, and so forth.

Did you ever watch a movie over and over and over? You probably enjoyed watching the same movie repeatedly. You find it to be a classic or an epic because it touched you in a way that you resonate with the story. You can sit there watching for days and you can repeat the script lines word for word. I'm not talking about a comedy, an action film, or horror movie.

I'm talking about the movie of your LIFE! Have you ever retold someone about an experience in which you were influenced, and it didn't work out as you thought it should have? The events unraveled this way and not that way because it was someone's fault; we believe it is because it is. It's because it's the pity party of our sad story.

When we start to realize we do not believe in ourselves, everything around us starts to flow like a waterfall – streaming down rapidly. Suddenly you start to wonder what happened in the course of that stream. Where did it occur and how did we miss the mark? Or, how come we feel? We wish to stay on the bay where we were more comfortable.

All the doubt starts to trickle down our body like if we felt that tremor underneath us, shaking us without realizing it is not our fault. Now we continue to blame others for our mistakes. We find all the excuses we make and try to justify our mistakes and bad choices by pointing a finger at another person or situation.

Do we not realize we are the creator of our life? How many of us think that the mind has power? Plenty! Do you really believe it? We have created the negativity in our life, and we are getting more of it. Did you ever look around your house and notice how many gadgets you have that are computerized? Are there gadgets that provide faults or errors, where immediately we do something about it to fix it ASAP?

Sometimes not, because of a lack of money, you say. What if your refrigerator power malfunctions? Do you not find a way to fix it before it spoils the food inside it? Absolutely! I remember it happed to me and I tried to un plug and plug and move things around like I'm fixing it. Eventually, I went to the store that weekend and purchased a new refrigerator. I was happy that I got a new one and it was time for the grocery store. How about the car that you are driving now, consider how hi-tech it is and how it contains all types of sensors to provide us directions, protections, and warnings. It tells if you are too close to a car, if you are not driving in your lane, and sometimes it even hits the brakes for you. There are beeps, or dings, to get you back on track.

It informs you and instructs you about maintenance as well – when the oil needs to be changed, or the air pressure in the tire needs to be checked, or if the engine needs to be serviced. We take immediate action because we want the car running smoothly on the road.

The point is all new technology has some type of indictor to give us direction for our next steps. Would you ignore these indictors to the point of malfunction? We are hi-tech people, and we want the technology to stay working and operational in all our devices; do we not want our life to be operational and working in the same way?

We are so eager to fix material things quickly and not discover, update, upgrade our inner-being – that is "who" we really are. Let me share a secret with you, which is not all that "secret". We have these emotional indicators that guide us. These indicators are strong about blaming, controlling, and being a victim of your feelings. They will attract your wants.

You are causing that relationship to fail because you have no understanding of YOU. You look at their behavior and want them to change, but you do not look at YOU in the mirror. You just want others to join the party of your life not going the way you want. Remember, as much as you want to change the person, you can't – because It is YOU who needs the change.

That person is a reflection of your thoughts. You are wishing to repair it, but you have no clue how. You will continue to not know how if you have made up your mind that others you are to blame. You have no belief to sustain that relationship at all. You made that mistake and now you would rather stay there and not make any improvement, rather than end a bad relationship that never went well.

Even if you moved on to the next relationship, it will cycle over again because it is another person with the same characteristics. In all actuality, the issue is you. Of course, you take account of their behaviors, and what they did wrong, and add it to your pile of frustration. You continue to allow others to guide you in your relationship because they have lost hope and you are agreeing that there is no hope.

When you change YOU, things will change! Thoughts are powerful, it is YOU, that will command yourself how you are going to feel. Are you unhappy? Are you unhappy about your career? Is there a career or a job you are seeking? You may attempt numerous times to send out your resume or get that interview. If you influence yourself with thoughts like "I have no chance in this world," or "Why would they pick me for the job when I do not have the experience or talents to do it?" then nothing will change.

If you do not believe in taking that course to help improve your skills and upgrade your resume, nothing will change. Be careful what you think, because it will become a reality as everything else has. Is someone is saying that you are too young or too old, do you not go after your dreams? If you start to believe others' words, you start to want something or someone to make that change in your life. You rely on others to fill that void; you anchor yourself to something or someone to feel complete.

I was having a conversation with a woman who was excited about this boy and girl relationship she was pursuing because it was a revitalized past relationship. Something she felt good about because she knew the person from teenage time. She always felt comfortable with the past relationship and was not making a new relationship with a man. She felt giddy about it. This guy just appeared and started to reminisce of old days. Then months passed and he disappeared without saying a word to her. He was probably not really interested in a long-time relationship with her. Why do I speculate that incident? It is because I am aware of how thing operate in a relationship with a person. I couldn't get feedback from him of why he bailed out. She was focusing on his behavior and words, and how he was always going to be with her. Unfortunately, she was facing contrast of her want or unwant instead of focusing on herself to bring her own happiness.

If this is you, then your unhappiness is on the exterior stuff. As that thing or person goes away you start to talk about the hurt, pain, and blame. You keep going this way, and you will get more of the same. Your thinking is giving you the same results and you accept it because it was taught to you. For you, this is the norm – to be like the mass of people that you were brought up around. If you always think that you won't get what you want, then you can never expect it.

Are you living unhealthy because eating or drinking is your remedy to healing or removing pain caused by an event, circumstance, or a person? Your family culture says so – and so it is accepted. Do you drink because it will make you manlier? Or, do you drink to forget the pain because that is the only way you know how to heal your emotion?

If any of these describe you, then you have not taken the time to use your thoughts. You have not considered how your thoughts affect your physical, financial, and relationship well-being. Are you grabbing that smoke - knowing what its influence is or what it can do to you in the long term? Have you have read the side effects but continue to think "It is what it is – I just cannot change my ways . . . this is who I am". You do not believe in changing your thoughts. You don't realize that it can help change your living health style.

If you believe there is a soulmate out there for you, or a relationship that can instill positive guidance or words of wisdom to your life, but the waiting is causing unhappiness, then you need to try a different tactic. Are you not born with a wonderful mind, and that full body conscious? That can change – with a gust of a wind. Remember, what you think about IS what you attract over and over. It is not the relationship that will make you a complete person – it is knowing who you are and all that you have become. Most people, however, think that their partner completes them. Everyone has a partner, so you want that. They complain that they aren't in a relationship now and speculate that they never will? They whine when their partner's isn't doing what they want, get mad. They watch other relationships and compare it to their own to find problems. All this could be avoided, if you as an individual knew YOUR desires and manifested them.

Remember, this is your reality not someone else's. Of course, you can bring others to the reality you all are sharing, and you all agree that it is truth. You can reminisce about the unhappy events that happened in the past. All back in the days, when you were this and that and how it was. That was before - not NOW. Are you going to retell the same story about your past and how negative it was when it is not serving you any good in the present? Do you continue to stay in your four walls where there is a door that is shut, closed, but unlocked for you to step out? You may believe you cannot go out there because you do not belong in the world. But, it is that bad habit of conviction that is keeping you from moving ahead – so you continue to stay that way and your results will surface to the reality you have created in your thoughts.

I was chatting with a friend, and she started to share her personal experience as a young girl: "You know, when I was little, I don't know what happened. I think I told you, my dad would try to carry me, and I didn't want him to. I believe since I was a little girl, I had resentment of my dad, because back then my mom had me at 16, but left me with grandma. I didn't grow up in a very loving environment, by me being the oldest cousin, a lot was expected from me. I had to help out with my other cousins, and then when my mom left - that affected me a lot. When I came here to United States, I thought I was finally going to be with her, but when she left again, my uncle adopted me. I cried every night for her. There's just a lot of things in me that I guess I haven't yet learned to let go, and a lot of times I get very emotional about things. But ever since I have been talking with you, I don't think of things like I use to. I would overthink things a lot. I'm trying not to be that way and just be happy, and for things not to really bother me."

Remember, if you are focused about being unhappy, you will continue to be unhappy, and it will be detrimental in your life. You can't get to happy or joyful if you continue to sharpen negativity in your feelings. Negative emotions have many attributes or characteristic such as frustrations, sadness, shame, fear, grief, depression, despair, envy, doubt, jealousy, and guilt.

Again, your inner-being and the physical you are a pole width apart. Your true self stays aligned with who you are, but when you allow conditions, circumstance, or events to dictate your feelings in a negative way, you no longer stay aligned and defer from your true self. We will get to that more in the next chapter.

Words of Appreciation & Hopefulness

I believe in me and I will continue to find clarity.

I know what I am about, and I will move forward and have fun.

Life is meant to be enjoyed and to continue prospering in my feelings.

The father in the story chose to change. You wanted the relationship to get better, but you do not take the time to develop you, so why do you want it to? Because you have different views, sights, visions, wants, and ideas that you want to match up with his or her thoughts. If one of you looks at the mountain and the other the ocean, you say you are different. This is because of your wants; however, you are wanting to push them to look your way instead of having them look at what's true with them.

You rumble with words back and forth of how a relationship works and how you convince the other partner this is the reality. They buy into your ideas because they care for you and they change, and now they love you. That relationship is unhealthy; you decide to stay because there is no way out. You allow verbal, or physical, or spiritual, or mental abuse. Are you not allowing those things in your life? Did you not choose to live that way?

Remember, you are the creator of your own growth, and you are getting more of what you want. That is matching what you are feeling or desiring; or whatever you want to label it to be. Is that what you are asking for? Are you attracting more of that in your life, and then blame someone's behavior to justify why you get more of that?

You can't grow because you do not look for the help you need. That mental state of mind is guiding you, but you do not listen. Yes, your intuition. Over and over you make the same mistake. Or maybe it is not a mistake – it's just a fallacy of your own interpretation of life.

You do not grow because you feel that is what life is. You blame your family member of your mistakes in life - you look at their past and judge them because of how you turned out. You find all the excuses to put them down, because you are not happy with your results. The easy way is to cop out, and to blame, and then bail out. You do not want to be accountable, so you stay stuck, and want someone to feel sorry for you.

You didn't get the grade you wanted - so you quit. Regardless how you see it, you will fail in everything if you just quit. Failure could be another way to understanding what you want in life, and you will choose not to go after your dream because you are tired of failing.

Continue to tell yourself you can't grow, and you will convince yourself that is the truth. Your attitude has won that battle of "You can't". You allowed your state of mind of "mediocre" to conquer you - therefore you want to lose.

Is your age a factor from stopping you to excel? Have you hit an age bracket that you are too "old" and now you can't grow because you feel you are ready for your retirement, and therefore no need to grow anymore? If you are allowing your age to command your failure, failure it will be. If you feel you can't learn from anyone, then you do not allow yourself to learn. We think that our age gives us the experience and we tell a younger person they do not know what life is. When in all actuality we can learn from the young ones how they want to live their life and not do what others are doing.

I was driving from picking up my son Daniel's friends; two brothers, and I asked them a question. "Do you like to be told what to do from your mother?" Both said, "NO". Of course, that was the answer I knew I was going to get. I do not know the percentage, but most young teenagers do not like to listen. Or we say that, because we know better and label them that.

They went on explaining that the mother doesn't want them to experience what she went through, and she is plunging her ideas to them as if they are really going to experience it. It is possible. If you continue to repeat the story over and over, they will live the life she has lived, and everyone else that is living it; and they will all say "I told you so."

A world of want and unwanted - you have chosen it and regardless which it was. Knowingly or unknowingly, your mind said "Yes" to want unwanted thoughts that you received. You are young and feel you do not need an answer to your compass. Your life is a cycle of mistakes. You must try them out for yourself to find out what works and what doesn't work. You go for what you want that will make you fly to your dream. If not, you will hit land, and soon enough you will program yourself to blame someone or something for your behavior because that is how you are. You keep telling yourself and you will fail, and you will.

You feel you did your duty as a man or woman, and no need to grow because of your hard labor. Your hard work has been your reality, and it was hard - so no need to continue to grow. Again, you will continue to stay where you are because the power of your thoughts gives you more of what you feel. Now you just want to go to a corner or lock yourself in a room and pout about all your past – of how you deserved this and that, and never got it.

Remember if you are not moving up then you are moving down. What is up or down? Do you not need both to understand what or how life works? How can you use both to balance your wants? If you are failing to be open-minded to trying something new - you won't grow.

A story I was told is that a lady named Evelyn ran into a woman at the store. The woman was asking Evelyn what she was doing different because she was looking young and vibrant. Evelyn responded, "I am redirecting my thoughts and knowing who I am." The woman started to complain about no growth in her life, her marriage was ending, and she'd lost her career because of negative attitude toward management.

This is the result of no growth, of failing to want to develop. You will attract want you think about. You add feeling to your wants, and you will get it. You do not want to grow because you are scared, you are afraid of changes. When you find your inner being within you, you will expand for growth, and opportunity, and find how good life is.

Words of
Appreciation and Hopefulness

Be inspired where you are going and march on.

Search what you want, and you will discover it.

Have fun in the process of your growth and enjoy.

CHAPTER 3

Do You Listen to Others?

When the feeling is wrong – the head thinks wrong.

A re you under the influence of listening to others? Do you permit the newspaper and the gossiping neighbors to do your thinking for you? Napoleon Hill once said: "Opinions are the cheapest commodities on the earth. Everyone has a flock of opinions ready to be wished upon anyone who will accept them."

Listening to others can lead you to an empty coffin. You can go in circles without realizing it. Listening to others means you are allowing another person to bid on your life. If you do listen, you will end up walking to the empty casket wondering how you got there. When that casket is closed, how will you achieve your purpose? There's no coming back!

"How did it all go wrong?" you will ask. You thought that person meant well for your life. Was it your mother or father, or a family member, or friends? Do you keep them in your life because you want to fail? Why not tell them to mind their own business because you need to find the true You? If you keep them there you will continue to get the same results you expect.

Yes, you do. You listen to others when their life is spiraling down. They have something to tell you because life is horrible for them. They want you to go down with them. You are allowing their energy to suck you in. You have heard of leeches - how they can suck your blood once they are on you and take nutrients from you – in the same way, that person is taking your energy and you know this is true -- and you let it happen.

You listen to family members that are so poisonous with negative words because they feel they know more about life due to their so-called "experience". Their tragedies, their ups and downs, and tenured years on the earth, so you obey what they tell you. You might say, "I do not listen to them, I do ignore them." But you are not making any positive progress – your actions are saying otherwise, and your talk is not aligning with your thinking; so, you are listening to them.

We need the contrast to understand what we are asking for in life. It gives us an opportunity to feel what want. They are still whispering in your mind, and you are listening because it is recorded in your mind.

You let that bad habit manifest in your soul. When they tell you to stay in that bad unhealthy relationship because it is the right thing to do, you can't find anything else. You stay in it for years because you listened to them – now you are regretting it.

I was talking to a friend about how bad her past relationship was and how the person used money to win her over because it was a way to bring them back to happiness. She thought that was how relationships operated. It became a habit so now it is a normal thing because you say to yourself and others, "That is life".

Or, have you heard that inner voice when you should not be in that relationship and you ignored it? You decided to stay there because you use excuses like "What would my parents think? What would my friends think? What would everyone think?" You are in the wrong relationship for the wrong reasons. You cannot decipher on your reasoning by what is right or wrong anymore, because you listen to the wrong you.

You have lied to yourself. Now you can't understand life anymore or how you should live life. You failed to have a great relationship with yourself, and you have allowed yourself to receive spiritual, mental, physical, and verbal negativity.

You are stuck, and you will stay stuck – no doubt about it. You do not think correctly, and you allow others to think for you – which makes you listen to their unsuccessful story.

They tell you about which career you should pursue because everyone in the family was doing the same thing. So, you listened. You listened because you are weak in thoughts. You allowed your thoughts to be weak because you did not want to develop them. Others thoughts impressed it so much in you; you believed it, and it became ingrained in you as a child. Therefore, you started to believe that it was your calling. Now you believe it is your purpose.

As you got older, you may think you were intended to have that life. And, because others thought that it was your purpose - you believed it. As a child you weren't thinking, so you got emotional about it, and allowed it to sink in emotionally and physically; and then it manifested. You probably never thought about it. When you were a child your conscious mind was open to receive everything – yes, everything. You received any ideas that your parents, friends, or the media said was so.

Listening to friends or family opinion because they know you better than yourself is absurd. You should know yourself. You should listen to your inner self. If you continue listening only to the negativity from others, you will fall right in with all the negative. Listening is a powerful influence if you continue to use it in a negative way, and it will create your life and ensure you will become a failure.

You are living in a world of variety. Once you decide and connect to your inner strength, there will be no split in what you want. It takes a while to decide because you need data. You see something you want and there you go after it. As an individual you think things can't be easy, you think you must feel the pain of hard labor. It is a process to coming to those decisions. You know what you prefer.

Other people may have convinced you that you just think you know, but you do not know, because they really know. They convince you that you should listen to them because they know. If you are not in touch with yourself enough to know your own preference, then you cannot connect to your inner power.

I received a call from my daughter Ailani, and she started to share her feelings about a situation that she was facing. This was a message she received and from an adult point of view:

I just wanted to say that I feel badly that you were crying last night - and the things you were crying about just makes me sad for you. However, I understand the reason you started to cry. It was because you were upset with Anissa because you both offered Juliet to come for a sleepover. Anissa said it was a backup in case your mom said no. Juliet's choosing to go there instead of your house is NOT Anissa's fault.

You are calling your dad every time Anissa upsets you and this has me really upset with you. Do you call him and tell him when you're a bad friend to Anissa? I know you don't!

You also call him to complain about your mom. Ligia may not be a perfect mom, but she is trying her best. Do you call him when she does nice things for you too? I bet the answer is, no.

I don't like that you are so quick to complain about her and other people, who love you so much. You need to learn that things are not only "GOOD" when it's convenient to and for you!

You said Monday, you didn't miss Juliet. So why now do you cry and complain to Blanca, that Anissa is taking her from you? You had all summer to ask her over and you didn't, not once!

You said our house is boring. So why you only want to come here when you have nowhere else to go? Or when other people are here?

Why do you say negative things about your mom only when you're mad at her?

Why do you say negative things about Anissa, when you "think" she did something wrong or when you are with your other friends?

All your actions have consequences!!!

You need to think before you act and speak. Oh, and by the way, Anissa is aware you talk bad about her behind her back. I've even been told about it. This is not how you are supposed to treat a friend. We both just ignored it because we love you and know you're young and naïve, and not always thinking right.

But I'm not going to treat you as her best friend anymore. You and she can stay friends, forever if you want, but it won't be the same.

A best friend does not behave the way you do. A best friend does not snitch her bad stuff to their mom and to other people. A best friend always has her best friend's back through good and bad times - in front of them and when they are not there.

Anissa has been hurt by you so much that she has been pulling away and treating you exactly the way you treat her. You have noticed because you said something to her. You don't like being treated the same way you treated her!

I'm glad Anissa has good enough friends who do not believe what you say about her, and to come tell me, when people are being mean to her.

In addition, the things you say about your mom can really affect her, because she is seen by other people as a negligent parent, and that's not right. She's your mom whether good or bad, you need to have her back, stay loyal, and respect her! Remember, she is human, and she makes mistakes, just like you do.

My only advice to you, is to think before you speak. I hope whoever you choose to be your next best friend isn't treated the same way you treat Anissa. All she did was 100% love you.

Oh, and hanging up on me last night, was not cool!

I thought about this message and I decided to intervene in a good father way: I want to let you know that Ailani can call me whenever she needs to, and she can let me know how she feels. It doesn't matter if you agree.

My position is to teach her how to see things in a different perspective. I don't teach anyone to be on one side. I teach everyone to see all aspects. Let's not go into who does what as a parent because I have done a lot, and made adjustments along the way, but I have tried to learn from my own steps of life.

I don't tell anyone all that I have done in my past. No one needs to know my business. My intention is to guide you to understand how life is and how you can have fun creating it, but it is your doing. Regardless who does wrong in your eyes, but I see it differently because that's what life's choices are based on – your own experience. I will get involved when I want to. I prefer to just stay by the bench and see how things are being created by each one's own experiences. Your experience is not the same as theirs. But you make your own choices, and you think you are right.

Again, I am here to see it as an experience and move on because we all make mistakes - that's what we are calling it and then use it as a lesson to improve. Today, Anissa and Ailani; my daughter are still good friends. And are in High School together, contrast bring the best in each one. If it is bad or good.

Words of
Appreciation and Hopefulness

Understand that everyone is on their own journey in life,
but that is not *your* journey.

Everyone comes into your life for a reason; to teach you,
and to learn about themselves.

You are a beautiful child of God;
do the best you can every day.

CHAPTER 4

Do You Lack Focus?

Failure is the inability to focus yourself to do your best.

Have you heard the quote, "Old person failure finally becomes tired, and makes their departure, failure cannot cope with persistence?"

Why are you still on the couch?

Why are you still on the bed?

Why are you still thinking about that idea and not executing?

You feel the energy and you do not want to make the step needed to change your life. Your negative state of mind is keeping you there because you see no other way out of your thoughts.

It could also be a good thing to realize what you want in life. You also have the positive state of mind that is You – where you can be happy no matter what you are doing. You have accepted your choices not to be disciplined. You suppress it in your heart - and your body is following what you told it to do. And now you are engaged in being a failure or feeling negative.

Are we labeled by others to think we are not focused because we are not pursing what they are doing? We need to meet their standard for them so that they think we are not lazy. Are you not aware that words are ideas and we get emotional about them? You don't have the capacity to reason why you limit yourself, so you stay where you are, in the dark, wondering why you feel paralyzed.

Have you examined yourself and decided you will always amount to nothing? Have you told yourself over and over you can't find a way out of your weakness – you are labeled with that title, so you stay in that state of mind? You are going in the opposite of who you are. Are you correct to feel that way?

Of course, you chose your thoughts – and you did accept those thoughts. No one else did it to you. However, you look around you and point at the stars, conditions, circumstances, and environment. You want to escape the reality, which started with YOU, but you need someone to be at fault, so you went ahead blaming your habits on someone or something for your inability or lack of interest.

When should you decide to be the judge of your mind? Judges makes decisions on power, purposes, method, discipline, and heavy training of cases. When will you be the lawyer of your own case? That lawyer will represent you; be your spokesperson; be a counselor on behalf of your inability.

Do you need jurors in your life? A juror discovers accurate facts of your thoughts, bad habits, and your actions, and will submit their results to find you guilty or not guilty. You are out of focus. Now you are bringing excuses for not tuning into yourself. Out of that you are feeling frustrated, confused, and lost. But if you tend to the opposite you will feel free, passionate, and loved. Your thoughts can take you to a direction that will get your emotions into feeling a positive or negative focus. Thinking of aligning yourself with your higher power can direct you to your focus of interest. If you keep thinking of those unwanted negative thoughts, they will continue to manifest as your experience, and you will wonder why you never really got what you want.

You will continue to wobble because you are not in ease. You need to shift your pattern away from your memory of the past. You have watched too many people lose focus in their experiences, so you drag it into your active thoughts. You have continued to write that story of why you are where you are. You keep talking about what was unwanted and you manifested what you are reminding to yourself. Procrastination is the wisdom not to force something you are unprepared to do.

Don't make it happen. Find inspiration not motivation.

Don't declare to remove motivation because it is more fun to act. Just find what is enjoyable and exciting. Why are you being so hard on yourself? A habit come from somebody else's habit and you are pleasing them and not learning from your inner being. You know your path, and they do not know your path. Are they dictating how you should live based on how they have been living their own experience? They will tell you they are correct based on their perspective and actions of life they have experienced themselves.

Have you ever tried to stay busy so others will see your efforts and tell you how hard you are working? Do you feel that is the recognition you deserve? If you look comfortable and making the job too easy, they will think you are undisciplined, or failing to meet their standard.

You know it doesn't matter what they think! Discipline is a command in your thoughts to be inspired or uninspired. If you line up with your inner self, get that power within you to come out, you will get a taste of that beautiful experience of focus, and tune into that life you want to experience.

I received a call from my son Daniel that his mother was upset with him because he wasn't home. He told me he was in his room taking a nap and his mom got on to him about not being home. Why did she assume he wasn't home? She checked his whereabouts on her iPhone and the location showed he was two minutes away at a friend's house. He told me he never left; he was napping. Did I trust him? Of course, I did. Because I trust me first, if he did lie, well that is not my problem. His behavior doesn't make me love him any less. Unconditional.

That day he wanted to go to the roller rink to skate with friends. He was getting a bit irritated that his mom assumed he left the house without permission. I suggested for him to focus on the good qualities about his mom. Kids tend to find the bad when the parents don't allow them out or when assuming something when it isn't true. The parents could be wrong, but parents rarely admit they are wrong, so they stick to their parental rules.

However, I did say to stay calm, meditate, feel good about the situation, and that all is good. I did tell him to ask her for her permission if he can go out to the roller rink. He did text her, but she responded a little too late for him go out with his friend. The idea was for him to focus.

When she came home, she wasn't upset. She asked him if he was interested going to Austin, Texas, the next week with his friend. Of course he said yes. He saw the good in the situation and stayed focused even though he didn't get out that day. The following week he did have an adventure with his friend and family for a weekend getaway. We spoke about it and he understood the meaning of focusing on something good and not looking at the problem as a problem but finding a solution instead.

I went to visit a friend at her mom's restaurant after finishing my Muy Thai class. As I sat there, my friend was eating lunch and her son was getting ready to leave for work. His mom was going to take him, but I exclaimed that I could take him to work which only took 10 minutes. The son started sharing his frustration and disappointment with his mom, how the aunt is so disrespectful to him, and he can't wait to leave. As I listened to the conversation, I gave him pointers about being happy now, in the present. I told him to not focus on the negative, because only he has control of how he feels. Yes, others will suggest something negative, such as cussing her out or giving her a knockout punch. But he knew that would not turn out well for anyone. I told him HE will take himself everywhere he goes. It is not so much about finding another job - it is learning to be happy because you are the creator of <u>your</u> life.

You can look at the situation as a learning curve and start to ask what you want. That is the contrast of life. You learn to choose. You can feel how it is to be at a work environment and how fun it is when everyone is in tune to their higher self. In this outcome, it doesn't seem pleasing because of the attitude of a person and you want to change the person. The changing you need to do is to turn your focus on you. Focus how you want to step into the restaurant and be the person you want to be.

Focus on not allowing someone else make you feel the opposite of your true self. The true love of you - will see the good in all. Soon enough you will find the job you want and the people that you will resonate with and have fun. He agreed that he will stay focused to feeling happy and enjoy his job. I know if he continues to stay active in the feeling-good place he will improve.

Words of Appreciation and Hopefulness

My daily mantra is "I AM FOCUSED!"

I am grateful for those around me, and for the positive experiences I have every day.

I appreciate those people in my life who are positive, and I reject the negative.

CHAPTER 5

Are You Under the Influence of Contrast?

Nothing is good or bad, except when our thinking makes it so.

Are you under the influence of thoughts of "You do not deserve it"? Are you focusing on the opposite side of the track? One track is positive, one track is negative. You have a choice to choose where you want to go. It is about a direction you want to be, so you can feel your best. But you choose FEAR, and it is capitalized because you broadcast it to everyone – therefore, that makes it your reality. And fear only means you are opposite of who you need to be.

Do you go around and pull everyone around you who will listen and let them know of your fear and your failure, so they can participate and encourage your thoughts? They probably do agree with you because they have gone through the same life train, so they understand your pain, frustration, sadness, and pity. You feel okay with feeling fear – and they empathize with you.

I have done some research in relationships and why people are getting more of what they want. They are attracting the things that they want to make their lives better. If they were in a relationship that didn't work out, it was because their feelings were their indicator of why it failed.

However, they are blaming themselves or they were blaming each other for it not working out. The mismatch was because each one wanted their partner to be a certain way; their behavior told them if they truly cared they would do A, B, or C. They were looking for conditions to make them happy, if the condition failed to meet their criteria, they didn't want the relationship. On the other hand, of course, you have a big fight about who is not doing what.

If you focus on you and fix the relationship within yourself, you will see how your relationship turns out in a positive way. Please realize you do not CONTROL anyone, and it is not your business to control them. You have no right to try to control anyone but yourself. Yes, you do deserve a relationship that is positive, but for it to be positive you need to change your ways of thinking. Your actions start from your thoughts.

Before you influence anyone to change, you need to change you. Also, a negative relationship is not so bad if you look at it as an opportunity to find what you want in your life. You may tend think they left you. Your focus should not be on if they left you, but that you are growing. You are finding out what is healthy for you to want, and you going to attract what you are seeking. You know it will be delivered to you based on how you think. Do you have to change your partner? Maybe not, and that's not what I am suggesting.

What I am saying is You changing you will get the results you want in your life. You, along with this other person, expanded the reality of your world. This is not hocus pocus. Think - if you say you think. Most likely, you are allowing someone else to do to the thinking for you because you can't seem to escape from that fear that is locking you up in an emotional jail. We know it is your imagination and you let it appear like it is truth. You have been practicing over and over the reality you are living in.

Remember that reality is comprised of the facts that you have developed in the days or years of what you think life is. You've been great to hold yourself there. Your focus has moved you toward that fear which has become your reality. Your reality becomes more and more of what you think. You are attending your facts from the start. What I am saying is that you have thought about being fearful or negative or things not going your way – and this means you blame others or things.

I remember Abraham-Hicks demonstrating the cork underwater - the cork can't just stay underwater alone; it has to be held underwater. Just like the cork, YOU hold yourself down by choice. You are choosing your thoughts and are getting those results in your life. Once you release the cork and let it float up, that is where the magic is. Actually, there is no magic at all. You are just no longer being held down with your negative thoughts. By understanding this, you will always win, and it is your choice either way. I remember I was holding unwanted thoughts that were bothering me for days because of someone saying something about my performance with whose perspective I disagreed. I kept hold tight the thoughts for days and it bothered me. I came to my knowing of who I am and I will continue to thrive because I have potential and I want to have fun in life and enjoy all that is being created so I let it go and now it feels good because it is not them that know my future but my inner being because I am receptive to success. Don't get others bother you, let go of the cork and stay connected with your high power or God and you will always win with love.

Remember it is not the person that you see that changes.

Because we have physical senses, we find the next person to blame. But the blaming is not your true self. You need to check yourself. It doesn't matter what anybody else does, what matters is – you are growing. And when you have that positive desire, and you maintain that positive side, you will always win. Also remember, if you get emotional about unwanted negative desires, you will get that too. You choose where you want to go.

This next section focuses on stores of individuals with a contrast in behaviors.

FIRST CONTRAST STORY

Olivia's Fight

I was introduced by a friend to a young girl, let's call her Olivia. Olivia was only 17 years old. At the time that I met her, I noticed she was wearing an ankle monitor. I wanted to know why she was wearing the monitor at such a young age, and I wanted to learn more about her story. I believed that she was wearing the monitor due to her behavior. Her behavior was perceived as bad by other people, and they felt that she was doing something wrong, which makes sense. But you must understand that not everyone will be pleased, or pleasant, about your actions.

Olivia told me that reason she had the ankle monitor on was because she got into a fight with another young girl. She said the other girl kept insulting her with words, and she felt that she needed to do something about it, so she hit her – and ended up beating her up. The parents of the girl she beat up were angry about the situation, and they called the authorities and slapped Olivia with a restraining order.

As I continued to have a conversation with Olivia, she was able to give me some more insight on what she had gone through. She was locked up in juvenile for over 265 days, for this incident. She ended up going back to juvenile detention for a second time for about a month after the first incident. I asked her if she liked going to juvenile since she had been in there, not once but twice. She expressed that it was not somewhere she wanted to be; however, being locked up did help her realize that she did not want to fall back into that trap and let it happen again.

We talked back and forth, and she told me she had gained some clarity and a good understanding of what she does want her in life - she does not like to be in jail. She enjoys her freedom; likes to be out and about; wants to take time to discover what life has in store for her; and wants to see what she can do for herself instead of going back to jail.

Olivia was not a troublemaker; she knew other people always viewed her as a troublemaker. Her mom, her stepdad, friends and family – all had bad views of her because of her bad behavior. Of course, since they felt this way about her, she sensed it, received it, believed it, and applied it. It became her reality, it led her to behave the way others expected her to behave.

Olivia did have trouble with her mother. Her mother told her, and believed, that she would end up in jail again - that she would always misbehave and never change. Her mother put that self-fulfilling prophesy in her head to help keep her on this track. But, Olivia's mother told her she loved her, and believed she was doing the best that she could do as her mom.

I feel that if her mother was in tune to who she herself was, meaning, if she did not look at conditions, but looked at life unconditionally, then she would love her daughter no matter what she did. She should give her some positive guidance, and certainly a lecture here and there, but not expect her to always be bad, and let her know that she still believes that her time to change will come.

If you feel out of tune with who you are, and KNOW your daughter will rebel and misbehave then, that's what you'll get. The self-fulfilling prophesy is that the daughter doesn't know any better. Because they believed she was bad, she believed had to be.

Olivia told me something she did four years prior at the age of 13. She probably believed she was a troublemaker at that time, and this was why she did this. She started taking mug shots pictures of herself being locked up. What she was doing was playing the role of seeing herself locked up – believing and know she would be in her future.

Fast forward to four years later when she was locked up and had fulfilled that prophesy – she now had a real picture of herself from four years prior.

She rehearsed being locked over and over again, so she got what she wanted. She manifested it, she desired it, and she made sure it happened.

People might say she couldn't desire this, but she did. She is the one who caused it. Other people were also part of the cause because, again she was thinking because of someone else's programming for her, and not thinking for herself. She let everyone else impact her decision because she felt negative. That is contrast in life.

Moving forward Olivia can create a new story for herself; she can create another mugshot but a positive one to show where she wants to go in life. She could be the president of a company, a lawyer, a doctor, whatever avenue she wants to go in life - but this time in a positive way. She can create a mugshot with her family, future husband and kids, anything she wants -- showing her having fun and enjoying life. Before you know it, maybe 10-12 years later, maybe sooner, she will see that picture on the wall and remember the conversation we had about this. Things can be manifested because she thinks intentionally about what she wants, and it will happen!

I don't see Olivia as a bad kid, instead I see her as a kid who is rebellious by trying different things that meet other's expectation of her. She will find what works out, what doesn't work out, but others will see it as right or wrong. You will encounter those people. We all hope that a young girl at this age does makes a transformational change down the road, but the decision is up to her. It's not up to her mom, stepdad, or friends – only she makes the final call.

We don't know what can happen five years from now, that will be her decision. Like I told her, I am here to give her an understanding, awareness, and an opportunity to see the path she wants to see so she can go to it and walk it.

It's okay to make mistakes or errors (that's all part of being human), but don't dwell on it or make it a big deal of it. Look at it as something you don't like and then transform and focus into something you like and move forward.

You will always have people who will try to tell you what's right and wrong and you will go back and forth. It's not a big deal, that's what life is and that's why we live in a life of contrast. There is always going to be a different perspective, different ideas, and a variety of choices. It's up to you to decide which one is better. Which one is worse? You'll figure it out.

Your own intuition will guide you to where you want to go. Your intuition will take you to the right path where you stay in tune to who you are. But whenever you disconnect, it will take you to the opposite and that's when you are walking on the negative road. That is the road where you will start to complain and start pointing fingers. And you may think life is over when it's not over, but you can cause it to be over if you continue pursuing that negative path.

Follow your bliss, be happy in the things you want to do, don't let anyone else be the judge of your decisions, or the judge of your thoughts because you can create the things, the life, or the relationship that you want. Stay tuned and stay connected to love

SECOND CONTRAST STORY

Mother and Daughter

Not too long ago, I had a mother and daughter both calling me to vent and ask for advice. I am very close to both these women. The mother (let's call her Alice) calls me and explains she is frantic and disappointed, and I asked her what is going on. She said that her daughter yelled out at dinner that she is gay and has been seeing someone for two years. "CAN YOU BELIEVE THAT?" Alice screamed. I said: "Yup." Alice was stunned and asked, "Why does this not surprise anyone?"

I said, "Alice, your daughter (let's call her Anne), has been in an all-girls sport team for about 10 years, heavily involved in the sport, and is now in college playing this sport." Now, I explained that I don't think that makes you gay, but her atmosphere and surroundings have only been with women. I was not trying to stereotype her but let her know I understood Anne's surroundings and lifestyle for most of her life growing up, and now Anne has turned 21.

Alice followed with these questions and I proceeded with my answers. I tried to be understanding yet firm.

"What do I do?" – Nothing.

"Did you know she was gay?" – No, but I'm not surprised.

"Why me?" – It's not you.

"Why my life?" – Umm, again this is not you.

"You don't understand, my daughter is gay, and will never have a real family."

Do you love your kids unconditionally? – "Of course, that is why I am so upset, I want her to finish college and marry a man and have a family one day. I have fought for her to have the perfect life."

I explained to her that I understand your daughter is choosing to love in a way you don't approve, and you do not know if she will have a family of her own. That she was showing her daughter conditional love and hate right now. That she believed there is something wrong with being gay, but Anne thinks it's ok. That being gay does not mean she will not marry and have a family. I had to help her see that she was showing her daughter that she will only love and allow her in your life and house if she followed her belief system.

Shortly after this conversation the daughter called me. She was calm and asked if I talked to her mother and heard the news. I told her I did and wondered how she was feeling.

Anne explained how she was both relived and worried her mother would not accept her and the person she loves. She explained she blurted it out at dinner as she was tired of her mother insinuating, she was a "gay ass." She explained that she has been holding this secret for more than two years, and I was surprised by that.

Anne mentioned that she and her mother have been had a rocky relationship for some time and she didn't know how to tell her. She recently went to visit her girlfriend (we'll call her Taylor) out of state and, finally, coming back from her visit they both made the decision that Anne should tell her mom at some point soon.

After spending time with Taylor, they had a great visit, and felt relieved to be open and accepted, and was hopeful she would receive the same feelings at home, but she did not.

I told Anne, there may need to be a time period to let things sink in with her mother. She explained that Taylor had felt it was her fault that Anne was having these issues with her mother.

I proceeded to explain that I believe nobody is at fault and no one did anything wrong in loving who they choose. No one is responsible for her mother's feelings and her mother's reaction, because she did nothing wrong. I advised to stay calm like she is and enjoy the love she feels and don't make any decisions or react according to her mother's feelings.

THIRD CONTRAST STORY

Past Experiences

One afternoon I received a text message from my friend saying she wanted to send a note to her daughter's father. It went something like this:

"I'm talking to my lawyer about the same things too. Off the record, please be mindful of what Valery has been going through when you let her be around your girlfriend. The reason we are now in court, Bryan, is because of the verbal, physical, and mental abuse that's been passed down from your grandfather, to your mom, and now to you.

Look at your past relationships and previous marriage – how you've treated all of us. I know you don't want that for Valery. PLEASE help me break the cycle like we planned, PLEASE!

She deserves to see and know that we are loving parents and that we love her no matter the person she becomes and that we will support her to speak, engage, and flourish. Please love her and direct her to positive things rather than tell her she can't.

I'm glad y'all are spending time together. She needs both of us. I don't want to take her away from you. I am protecting her from what your mom, your past relationships, and I have experienced with you, and to break that cycle in both of our families. It's your culture - it's hurtful. Please help me, Bryan.

Love her, be kind, and be mindful of your words - she's still learning."

Physical Attributes

Devon P. shared an interesting story about one of his older brothers' transgender journey. Devon grew up in Texas and he is the youngest of 10 children. The brother, a male, mentioned in this story was known as "Jon" since birth, but he felt more comfortable identifying with a gender different than the one assigned to him. His story is a perfect example of how we live in contrast.

Around the age of 25 Jon realized that he wanted to move forward with his gender transformation to live life as a female and undergo a medical transition so he could live a happier life. Jon was under the influence of his own decisions to do what made him happy. He did not allow others to convince or dictate what he wanted. He took a risk and did what he felt he wanted to do. This was HIS calling.

Jon, now living as a female, returned home after undergoing surgery to face his parents and family. He was approached by his mother first and greeted her with excitement and said the words – "Hi Mother".

She obviously knew all her children so at first, she was a little confused and wondered why this woman was calling her Mom.

His father didn't think much of what going on, but once he realized the situation he was also taken by surprise.

Devon was around 10 years old at the time and he clearly remembers the events that took place. He sensed familiarity in this person, but it took him time to figure out that his brother was now Stephanie, a female. Stephanie's family supported her decision although it took some time for them to accept it, instead of trying to manipulate him to change.

Stephanie knew what she wanted all along to find happiness. With her transformation she found her identity and along with that came joy, happiness, and a lifelong partner. Fast forward to 40 years later, they are still together as a couple despite being "different" or labeled as "others". These situations happen every day. Don't let others influence your happiness and stop worrying about what other people think.

The Alabama Trip

As I was driving back from Houston with my daughter, I asked her about her recent trip to Alabama that she took with her mom, aunt, and cousin Milton. Her initial response was "drama"; however, she enjoyed the trip. It was a new place for her to explore and she was excited to go.

Her cousin on the other hand wasn't so excited – which upset his mother. Milton is a 15-year-old boy who has lactose intolerance issues, which causes him to be in the restroom for minutes, or hours, after eating or drinking certain things. Although he has been to the numerous doctors, he still does not have answers to what is causing this. It's out of his control. He was forced to go on this trip by his mom, and she wanted everyone to enjoy the trip and have a good time.

Milton's family had made a list of things to do while on the trip – like going to the beach, but Milton had no desire to do anything. He knew he would be stuck in the hotel room when he would have been more comfortable just staying at home with his brother.

That didn't mean his mother would have failed to enjoy herself on this vacation with her sister and niece, but without him. The adults looked at this as a negative situation, but it really wasn't. Milton was content staying at the hotel figuring out what to do on his own to keep himself busy and happy while the others could go out and enjoy themselves and have fun.

He knew how to keep himself occupied and if he wanted to join the group later, he could have simply reached out to them so they could come pick him up or meet up somewhere. Instead of getting mad about his behavior they should have let him be and enjoyed themselves.

As parents we expect our kids to do everything we want to do, but we cannot force them to enjoy it. It's okay to leave them alone and continue to do what you want. This pattern causes the parent(s) to be upset and most likely not enjoy themselves as much or restrict them from doing something they would like to do. In this situation, Milton did not want to be there or do certain activities. That doesn't mean the others had to miss doing what they wanted to do; yet still have fun. Everyone was happy doing their own thing.

In our day to day life we tend to play the blaming game by letting someone else's behavior dictate our feelings. We all have our own choices and we are in control of our feelings and how we view situations.

Kids, just like adults, have the decisions to make their own choices. As parents, we need to guide them to understand this process and this is also something they will learn through their own life experiences as they get older.

Work Differences

Relationships can be one-on-one as well as one to many and they can happen anywhere - at home, at work, even at the gym. A relationship can be defined as gathering together, working together, or helping one another in a collaborative and harmonious way.

There is always going to be contrast at work. Contrast is something that one is desiring, when somebody likes or doesn't like something.

This story is about contrast at work in an IT department at an organization where I was previously employed. As a whole, this department is a team. But this team is also divided, let's say Team A and Team B. It was apparent that these teams did not like each other because one team's ideas were different from the other team's ideas.

During their technology discussions, investigating technical issues, working on technical solutions, and sharing ideas on how to resolve these issues, these two teams had many differences. They did not get along. I remained neutral and enjoyed observing the different ideas being presented and seeing both sides of the talent and skills. In my eyes there was not right or wrong. Sometimes ideas do not need to align, and you then begin to see others negatively and not to their full potential. When you are not in alignment with yourself you tend to judge others.

The managers of these teams constantly disagreed; they could not align their ideas. One day the manager of Team B made the decision to leave the organization due to some information he heard was leaked against HR policy from a Vice President. His departure trickled down and other members started to leave too. They wanted to move on and look for other opportunities elsewhere. I believe that if each member knew what they wanted they could have gotten it, within time.

I had the chance to meet up with the former employees to sit down and listen to their stories. All of them came to the table with a negative state of mind about the situation. Again, I enjoyed listening to conversations of them discussing their issues, concerns, problems, complaining, and blaming others. People can change jobs and face the same situation at another organization. It's how YOU see life and how you want to see it. We are observers of life and reality. You create your own reality. You can move on or leave even an organization even if you are happy. It's all about your attitude. It's You; you create the place; the individual could be the one creating the problem.

One employee on the team left after serving 15 years! He felt that people did not see him the way he wanted to be seen. Why is it that we tend to focus on the behavior of others? We cannot change the behaviors of others. Focus on what you want you want to do, enjoy what life can bring you and look at things with a different perspective. Are you under the influence of how others see you and talk about you? Or under the influence of staying aligned with how you believe in yourself. You're doing is your own doing, it's an inside job.

Stay tuned in, stay connected and plugged in to who you are. Feel worthy of who you are. Don't worry about anyone else, allow things in your life to flow. Enjoy life and continue to let things flow, life is all about improving. Too often we tend to get caught up in the drama - sure it can be difficult to not be around drama, but you don't have to get involved, it's all in how you see or analyze things.

Be happy and go for what you want!! Stories are shared because we will have contrast - it is how we will perceive or get emotional about the situation if we make it simple or colossal for our experiences.

Words of Appreciation and Hopefulness

That feeling of abandonment from family members,
does not define who you are.

Feeling that no one demonstrated the right path for you,
means you find your own path.

They told you "Money is evil" so you don't deserve more,
so you believe what you have is all you can get.

Believe you are worthy, and don't buy into negativity.

Don't let the idea transfer, be the entire pillar
of your failure . . . or your future.

CHAPTER 6

Telling a New Story

Thomas A. Edison failed 1000 times, and a new story was born.

A re you under the influence of creating a new story in your life? You are the leading edge of your perspective, the leading edge of your life, the leading edge of your thoughts, and the leading edge of your creation. You have permission to direct your feelings and emotions to greatness.

You can't change your family or friend's point of view. You can observe their behavior or see the results they are getting by their actions, or by them sharing their words. You can only change your view with thoughts that create your reality. You have the power of the Mind.

Have you not realized you witness your thoughts to things? Look all around you. We are constantly creating material things; you are physical – and that does make you a material being or human person. However, look at the house you live, the friends you choose, or the relationships. Consider that significant person or families from both sides, mother or father and that is the power of the thoughts - that we call ideas and how you get emotional – and it manifests to physical.

We do the same when we use our internal sensors; which are our basic senses: hear, smell, taste, sight, and touch. One that we have been talking about is the emotional GPS which give us the feeling of being happy and appreciative of who we are. We can desire to want to feel happy about life. You can, and you should, create the joy and happiness you want. Your thoughts are what creates your life. You call it focus.

When I made the decisions to pursue my home schooling to achieve my high school diploma, I was focused. My intention was to get that diploma! All I wanted was to be able to say I did graduate. When I got the diploma, the next step was for me to get to the next level for my Associate's degree in Computer Networking. Because when you are in tune to ideas – you create that desire of what you want – and you can work to fulfill that desire. Your emotions are the indicator what you are creating.

It is your duty to feel wonderful and happy about your life. Exploring, deciding, preferring, creating, and becoming. There is a solution. We are solution-based individuals. If you can focus on that new idea, you will see the transformation happening. You are creating new habits. When I started to dive into my academic classes, I was a great slave to learning – and I was having fun!

Do not let the conditions, circumstances, or events decide your feelings. The only power we have over those things is how we feel with our emotions and where we want to go. Don't let the outside interfere with your beliefs.

When I did get my degree, it was a challenge getting a job in the IT field. Everyone is looking for the experience. The only thing I had was my belief and attitude knowing I will land the job I wanted. At the time I was just thinking of time, when would I get my chance or break, I just felt (emotions) and remembered to not listen to the outside circumstances but listen to my inner voice. This chapter is dealing with You and only You. You have it in you to allow yourself to feel good. Do you not see you can create a new story?

My daughter Ailani loves to go to the Chinese buffet because she can select the meal she wants. I do not tell her what she must pick out – she chooses what she wants. Even times when I wonder why she is getting (what I think) is that nasty food; I remember it is her choice. Again, it's her enjoying the selections which she wants, because it gives her a great feeling eating it and learning how to get what she wants.

You have options as you pick the food you eat, the car you drive, the house you live in, the friends you want, the clothes to wear; these are selections of things you pick. These things are conscious (awareness) or unconscious (not aware).

The beautiful thing about contrast is that you know what you want and do not want. Nothing is wrong, it is just a focus of attention on how we are looking at life. Jesus said in Matthew if there is a different perspective with someone's ideas to turn your cheek and refocus your perception, because you and no one else has any control of what someone does in their life.

You go for the things you enjoy or find appealing for your taste. Give yourself the benefit of the doubt. When I was open to receiving and knowing I can live the life I wanted, it wasn't about the material things, but it was who I really am. I started to realize it is not conditions, circumstances or environment that would make me joyful. It was my change of thinking and getting the correct feeling of being happy. I knew that I would know the truth of who I was meant to be then my conditions, circumstances, and environment changed too.

We all have turned on the AM/FM radio on to listen to our favorite station, and what we listen to we have a vibrational match to what we want to hear. The frequency we are hearing – and feeling – is what we are wanting. If that is a sad song, love song, or a happy, joyful song, we are a match to what we emotionally are sending and receiving, and we get what we want or not want.

As a person that understands wireless technology, because I am an engineer in that field, we use the words frequency, which means a signal that goes back and forth, one device to another device. You need a master and a slave. You must go to the master controller and make the change for the slave (also called the client) to accept the changes. We have access to change the channel to the station we want to feel. No one knows better than you.

As I am sitting down, I was reminiscing about a time when I was about 14 years old. At that time, we carried pagers (we young kids called them beepers) in those days. Now we have cell phones that send text messages and can surf the internet. Everyone is carrying a phone - grandparents, parents, children, and my pet dog Lexy. (OK, so I'm joking about that one. I think I will run the other way if that happened!)

Consider how much we have evolved in the area of technology and it is increasing fast with marketing what's new and hot at the store. You notice all the upgrades and new version of this or that. We all want the new gadgets and things that are coming out and how much it means to have the new phones or the new things that everyone is having. It makes us feel great when we have it and how it makes us feel like we are part of something unique.

Do you see that you are directing your thoughts to that thing and when you do you get emotional about it? You are placing so much attention to it that it is driving your emotions. That is a great feeling that you can tune your feelings from your thoughts. You see what you can offer – it is the feeling of feeling good. I am not here to suggest you feel good about the condition nor things, but for you to know who you are and to be happy who you are. That's because there are no things, or anybody that can make you feel good.

We came forth to give birth to what we want to create. The value of contrast is to understand negative and positive. Negativity provides an avenue to seek the opposite what we are desiring, and we go ahead with positive emotions because it makes us feel joyful.

Your infinite intelligence (or whatever you would like to call it) is your guiding system when we are in love – is because we are in love with who we are. Yes, you have a choice to feel good. You are where you are because of you feeling what you are attracting.

We are creators of the technologies that are being manifested. The new phones. The game stations. The new cars. The new businesses. From the billboard to the media advertisement, they tell us that it is high quality and much better than the last; then years later, they repeat the same thing. Once again, it's come and purchase this phone, or game station, or new car because there is always new development for us to want. We are desiring new things all the time because we are creators of our life. We want to live to see new things because we are evolving human beings. Regardless of the old or new things, what matters is how you feel about being you.

Be happy because you are happy before the things come. We love to collect data and many options to look for the positive of what we are witnessing in our life. We are the attractive of what we are attracting. Yes, we should put our life first and that is to be happy.

CHAPTER 7

Creating Your Story

Be the master of your destiny.

You and I will step in or step out of contrast all the time,
so let's look at those steps.

LET'S LOOK AT THE FIRST STEP:

Desire, ask, sift, sort, set preferences, choose the good, find the diamonds in the rough, look for rainbows through the clouds, wishing, thinking positive thoughts, dreaming, defining, refining, options, deciding what you like, wanting, question the thoughts, find the joy.

LET'S LOOK AT THE SECOND STEP:

Universe, source, God, Vortx, listening, getting answers, saying yes, looking forward to the alignment, finding the way, gets cracking on the steps toward, receives the launched rockets of desire and never looks back, the vibrational reality assembles or comes back together, cooperative components gather, universe aligns to your desires.

LET'S LOOK AT THE THIRD STEP:

Allow, feel the good, trust, have fun, be love, enjoy yourself, be ready to be ready, let go, have faith, stay open, be blissed out in the journey, stay tapped in and turned on, find the feeling place of appreciation, presence in every moment, chilled, receiving answers, quieted mind, discovery of unfolding, hold the space, energy, or vibration for everything in your desires.

LET'S LOOK AT THE FOURTH STEP:

Get good, stay consistent, know all is well, care about how you feel, awareness, stay awakened to the process, give time and energy to what feels good, expectation of the unfolding, unconditional, riding the high-flying disc.

What Life Could Propose

Think about what we have talked about so far:

Are we not under the influence of our thoughts?

Are we not under the influence of a just life?

Are we not under the influence of our experiences?

Are we not under the influence of external things?

Are we not under the influence of family affairs?

Are we not under the influence of friendships?

Are we not under the influence of what is around us?

How are we allowing those influences to affect us in a positive way?

If we could just understand that we have the potential in us to do the things that we enjoy doing, then we should go do it! We don't need someone else's opinion, we don't need to ask for permission, and we don't need to consult with someone else to ask them what they think we should do. What we should do is learn to be influenced from ourselves first then continue move forward.

Things will move forward in life and things will move forward in the things in you want. Don't let other factors affect you, whether its relationships, money, or external things.

Staying focused on the things you like will not only help you in enjoying your life experiences, but it will also help you to enjoy what you are creating with others who share the same emotional feelings or what we call good energy or good vibes. When you share the same good feelings as another person, it's because at that moment you are feeling good and the other person is also feeling good, so you are attracting one another.

In life, it is not necessary to tell people your goals or what you envision for your future, your goals are all going to come, your goals are going to happen, just enjoy what happens during your journey. Enjoy what you see today in the present and have fun with it. Don't have a negative outlook just because things do not turn out the way you want them to, in due time things will work out. Once you set your mind to something you are going to achieve it, you are going to manifest it because you are the creator. But in between you are going to go through different barriers.

For example: you leave your home at a certain time of day, it could be at a peak time, and many others are also leaving at the same time so you may encounter heavy traffic but, in the end, you will get to your final destination. Factors such as stop lights or signs, accidents, construction, or pedestrians might slow you down. You know you are going to encounter these barriers so why not just enjoy the ride. Just as in life, things will get better because what you are thinking will create your experience.

It is inevitable that you are going to have negativity in life, this is not necessarily a bad thing, it could be fun because it's going to give you contrast which creates an opportunity for you to decide where you want go, what you want to do, and what you like and don't like.

Another example is a chef, chefs like to cook great food. They want people to experience their choices of ideas, ingredients, and how they put things together. You are the chef of your life, you create your own ideas, you put together your own ingredients so people can see what you are bringing to this earthly world.

In technology there are people creating software that we can use to interact with each other. Isn't it interesting that the human beings are the creators of the software? It's not the software or the technology that creates us, we create it! This incredibly technology comes from our thinking and our thoughts. Technology will never take away from jobs, it just creates more opportunity.

Look at fitness, it is a fun activity, you can build your biology and the way you want to look. It's all in your thinking, your thoughts create your biology so your biology changes when you start to know what you want. When you start to find inspiration, you start to get motivated. Therefore, you associate working out with changing your biology then your biology changes because of your desire to change. So therefore, you are changing your physical appearance by how you want it to look, you are the creator of your body whether you know it or not.

This is a book intentionally based on how to enjoy life – to have fun, learn, and how to go on to experience the life you want. This book gives you ideas which allows you to understand that we are all here together creating things and having fun with it. We are the elite individuals that will continue to make things happen in our own life.

Don't let others effect you because they are doing something different then what you are doing, we are all here to do our own duties. What is right? What is wrong? Everything can be right or wrong, it is all about perspective, how we perceive things, how we were taught, or it could be a habit we created. Just enjoy life! Enjoy, enjoy, enjoy! When you repeat this action then you will have joyful moments. When we repeat things over and over, we start to create them and enjoy what life can bring.

Life is ready to bring whatever you want, are you ready for it? The world is an equal opportunity for both the person who is thinking positive and the person who is thinking negative. What are you thinking about that is making you happy? Are you finding inspiration then following motivation, and calling it action, grinding or hard work when it's really just simple joy to do what you want? If you are not happy then go find happiness, then everything else will come to fruition.

Taking Inventory of Your Desires

Desire is the flow of wanting things without having to commit to pursuing them. It is the idea that you can change your mind based on the current feeling you are having. Out of desire it can transform to a goal or a dream.

I am so happy and appreciative now that _____

_____

_____

_____

_____

_____

_____

_____

_____

Ideas to
Act Upon Immediately

These are the top ten ideas that I will act on immediately to move me toward my desires:

1. _____

2. _____

3. _____

4. _____

5. _____

6. _____

7. _____

8. _____

9. _____

10. _____

Personal Exercises to Reach My Desires

These are the activities I will do every day as personal exercises to reach my desires:

1. For 15 minutes meditate and do not think of anything. If you do, get back to not thinking and allow yourself to just let go.

2. Write your affirmation, read your affirmation, or listen to your affirmation.

3. Read your goals, re-write your goals, add more goals and think about your goals.

4. Read books that will inspire who you are meant to be.

5. Physical exercise, lifting weights, jogging, swimming, walking et cetera.

6. Participate with harmonious groups where you can benefit and learn from each individual.

(Remember this is an idea of what you can follow, or you can be creative and create your own steps of exercise that will make you feel wonderful.)

THANK YOU!

I hope this book has brought some new ideas into your life and how the change is always within. I appreciate you allowing me to take the time to share my life experience from my point of view and how it is always evolving for the better. I see life has an opportunity to create it how I want it and as well with others to explore our different tastes of life. With much appreciation, "Thank you" from my heart that this book has served us today and many more days to come to realizing our full potential and how our inner calling is always listening to us when we are available to quietly listen.

Luis C. Delgado

Made in the USA
Middletown, DE
22 September 2022